Beginning Biographies

Helen Keller
Miracle Child

Audrey Peck

PowerKiDS press™

NEW YORK

Published in 2013 by The Rosen Publishing Group, Inc.
29 East 21st Street, New York, NY 10010

Book Design: Katelyn Londino

Photo Credits: Cover, pp. 4, 21 Hulton Archive/Stringer/Archive Photos/Getty Images; p. 5 Dr. Gilbert H. Grosvenor/Contributor/National Geographic/
Getty Images; pp. 6, 13, 14 Walter Sanders/Contributor/Time & Life Pictures/Getty Images; p. 7 commons.wikimedia.org/wiki/File:AnneSullivanMacy.jpg/
wikipedia.org; p. 8 commons.wikimedia.org/wiki/File:Helen_Keller_with_Anne_Sullivan_in_July_1888.jpg/wikipedia.org; p. 9 Rolls Press/Popperfoto/
Contributor/Popperfoto/Getty Images; pp. 10, 16, 19 Library of Congress; p. 11 Hulton Archive/Stringer/Hulton Archive/
Getty Images; pp. 12, 15 Topical Press Agency/Stringer/Hulton Archive/Getty Images; p. 17 Rollie McKenna/Photo Researchers/Getty Images; p. 18 MPI/
Stringer/Archive Photos/Getty Images; p. 20 Nina Leen/Contributor/Time & Life Pictures/Getty Images.

Library of Congress Cataloging-in-Publication Data

Peck, Audrey.
Helen Keller : miracle child / Audrey Peck.
    p. cm. — (Beginning biographies)
Includes index.
ISBN 978-1-4488-8824-5 (pbk.)
ISBN 978-1-4488-8825-2 (6-pack)
ISBN 978-1-4488-8593-0 (library binding)
1. Keller, Helen, 1880-1968—Juvenile literature. 2. Deafblind women—United States—Biography—Juvenile literature. 3.
Deafblind people—United States—Biography—Juvenile literature. I. Title.
HV1624.K4P43 2013
362.4'1092—dc23
[B]
                            2012010468

Manufactured in the United States of America

CPSIA Compliance Information: Batch #WS12RC: For further information contact Rosen Publishing, New York, New York at 1-800-237-9932.

Word Count: 414

Contents

An Important Woman

Helen Keller was a strong and smart woman. She became a **famous** writer and speaker even though she couldn't see or hear.

Hard Times

Helen was born on June 27, 1880. She grew up in Alabama. Helen could see and hear until she was 19 months old.

In 1882, Helen got very sick. After her illness, she became **blind** and **deaf**. This made life very hard for Helen.

A Helping Hand

Helen needed a teacher to help her. In 1887, a teacher named Anne Sullivan came to live with Helen's family.

Anne was 20 years old when she started to teach Helen. She was a great teacher. She was once blind like Helen. An **operation** helped her see again.

Helen didn't know any words. Anne taught her
how to spell words with her hands. This is called
sign **language**.

Anne helped Helen learn what words meant. Helen touched things. Then, Anne spelled their names on Helen's hand. This is how Helen learned the words for things.

Helen learned a lot during her time with Anne. She learned 30 words in one day! Helen loved learning.

Learning at School

Helen was a very smart girl. She went to school for the first time in the fall of 1889. Her school was in a big city called Boston.

Helen couldn't see words, but she still learned to read.

She read by feeling raised dots. The dots spelled words.

This is called braille (BRAYL).

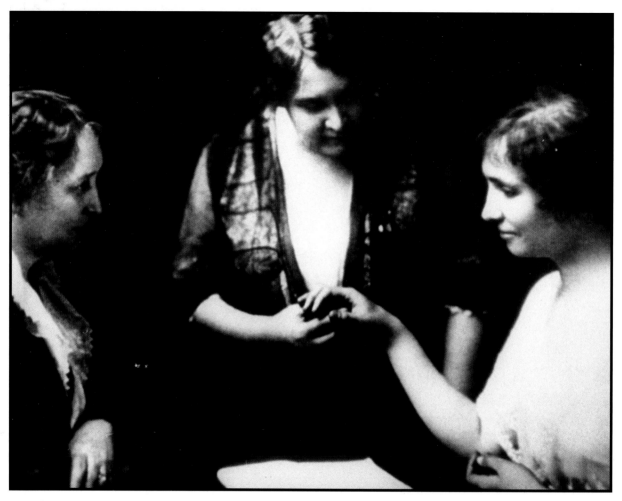

Helen used her hands to learn other things, too. She learned to talk by feeling her teacher's mouth. She felt how to make sounds.

Helen did well in school. In 1900, she went to **college**.
Helen became the first blind and deaf person
to finish college.

Writing and Speaking

Helen liked to write. She wrote her first book in 1902. It's called *The Story of My Life*. People still read it today!

Helen wrote 10 more books during her life. She wrote about being blind and deaf. She showed others what life is like for blind and deaf people.

Helen traveled around the world after she finished college. She visited 39 countries! She spoke to people about her life.

A Teacher and Friend

Helen always traveled with Anne. She was Helen's teacher and friend. They lived together until Anne died in 1936.

Helping Others

Helen lived until she was 87 years old. She died on June 1, 1968. She helped many blind and deaf people during her life.

We can all learn from Helen's life. She followed her dreams even though she was blind and deaf. What are your dreams?

Helen Keller's Life

1880 Helen is born in Alabama.

1882 Helen becomes blind and deaf.

1887 Anne starts teaching Helen.

1889 Helen goes to school for the first time.

1900 Helen goes to college.

1902 Helen writes her first book.

1936 Anne dies.

1968 Helen dies.

Glossary

blind (BLYND) Unable to see.

college (KAH-lihj) A school after high school.

deaf (DEHF) Unable to hear.

famous (FAY-muhs) Very well-known.

language (LAYN-gwij) The way a person writes
and speaks.

operation (ah-puh-RAY-shun) An action performed by a
doctor on a person's body to help that person get
healthy again.

Index

Due to the changing nature of Internet links, The Rosen Publishing Group, Inc., has developed an online list of websites related to the subject of this book. This site is updated regularly. Please use this link to access the list: **www.powerkidslinks.com/bbio/helen**